I dedicate this book to all people who are seeking a way to successfully navigate a fulfilling career and a meaningful personal life at the same time. My hope is that this book inspires you to believe that true work-life integration is both possible and well worth the effort it takes so that you come away ready to go ahead and get after it!

TABLE OF CONTENTS

DISCOVERING THE SECRET TO WORK-LIFE INTEGRATION

B alance. It's a topic anyone serious about growing their career has probably thought about more than a time or two. With so many people facing competing demands at work, at home, and within the community, it's no wonder that some of the best-selling professional development books promise to deliver that elusive unicorn of work-life balance. And that's exactly what it is: a unicorn. It doesn't exist.

That's the bad news, of course. But there's also good news: you can have a fully satisfying life and career, even in the absence of that mythical balance. You *can* have "work-life integration." Work-life integration involves blending both personal and professional responsibilities. When you are able to properly coordinate your schedule and responsibilities, you are more likely to experience satisfaction in all areas of your life. Emphasis is on outcomes and quality of work, not about when and for how long the work is being done. Rather than trying to make sure every aspect of your life gets equal time, what if you could think about it in terms of making sure every aspect of your life is *fulfilling*, no matter how much time it gets (or doesn't get) on a daily or weekly basis?

In my nearly 30-year career in corporate America, I worked incredibly hard, sacrificing mightily along the way— and yet, I still believe that my experience was both rewarding and very much worth it.

Like all bright-eyed and ambitious young adults, when I started my professional career, I had one priority: I wanted to make a lot of money. At the time, I really didn't understand the true meaning of a lot of money, nor could I define it. However, I was willing to make personal sacrifices, poor decisions, and put personal values aside to pursue my dream.

For more than twenty years, I seemed to be *the guy* at my company, the poster child for success and fast-track promotions. I moved up the corporate ladder so quickly, you might have thought I was on a career advancement escalator.

But there was a personal cost to it all. I made sacrifices as I gave the best years of my life to the company. I relocated my family—frequently—all across the country. I also traveled regularly. I missed school plays, parent-teacher meetings, and often felt like I was on the outside of the special relationship my daughters had with their mother as a result of her playing the single-parent role so often.

And yet, I can honestly say that my career success was fulfilling, even though there were significant tradeoffs. As one of the company's shining stars, I was well-compensated with salary, bonuses, and company stock—which allowed me to pay my daughters' college tuition.

The further into my career I went, the more I began to understand that work is most fulfilling when it is integrated into life as a whole, and that's where the Life Fulfillment Framework comes in.

In the pages to come, we'll unpack this Framework. Instead of looking at a simple 50/50 work-life balance proposition, I'll show you how to maximize your life fulfillment in five key areas: Family, Faith, Finances, Fears & Challenges, and Friction. These five areas deserve special attention throughout your career at each stage of The Career Life Cycle. I'll share my personal experiences and lessons learned in each stage and offer guidance to help you successfully navigate your own career experience.

———

CHAPTER ONE

FAMILY

I t's hard to overstate the importance of family in your career. At different times in the Career Life Cycle, you'll have different family concerns, and oftentimes these concerns are ongoing. In my case, I always had concerns at the back of my mind surrounding my decision making, how to juggle career and family, self-doubt, and questioning the stability and longevity of our marriage.

I attended Jackson State University where I got my degree in finance. That's also where I met Bobbie, who was also a finance major. After I graduated in 1986, my next step was to serve in the United States Army, and so when Bobbie and I eloped in 1987, she became a military wife. I was stationed at Ft. Hood, where we had an exciting life but very little money. We were determined to make it work.

There was a lot of uncertainty—I might even say fear— at this time in our life. This was my first real job, and I knew I had to keep it to be able to take care of my responsibilities as a new husband and provider. With no extended family close by, it was just Bobbie and me. We had to learn how to depend on each other. We had to make it together as true partners.

Except oftentimes, we weren't *actually* together. When you're in the cavalry or infantry in the military, you're often not home. You're participating in field training exercises for several days or even several months. So it's important to have a close and trusting relationship. If you don't, the marriage is not going to survive. I would say the same is true for anyone starting out in a career and trying to integrate work and family life, but the military has an especially high divorce rate.

And then our first daughter, Tiffany, was born—a total game-changer. It went from being just the two of us to the three of us. How were we supposed to raise this child when we both had to work? We realized that one of us needed to become more of the homemaker, and the other, the primary financial provider. That realization proved to be a pivotal moment in the family, as was the fact that Tiffany was just three weeks old when I deployed to Iraq for a year during the first Gulf War. I didn't come back until she had already turned one.

Thankfully, the military is family-oriented. When a soldier is gone for months at a time, the military offers family support. Army wives are a tight-knit group, so Bobbie was able to get strong support when she started to feel overwhelmed. But missing a year of my firstborn's life did not sit well with me. I knew as soon as I returned from Desert Storm that I would have to make a change. That's when I began my journey into the civilian world and moved to Wisconsin.

We were fortunate to be part of the Oscar Mayer Division of Kraft, a company that, at the time, was also family-oriented. Their values and beliefs aligned with our family values. We knew everyone and felt like they were family. Bobbie knew other spouses with whom she developed friendships and a strong support system. The company hosted events every year, like Christmas celebrations and summer activities for kids, which helped make it feel like the right fit for our family.

Even as African Americans in Wisconsin back in the early '90s, when the minority population was less than 3%, we never felt different or like outsiders. The community and our church family warmly embraced us.

However, one key to advancing with a company is being willing to relocate for promotions. We eventually were tapped to moved to South Carolina. It was there that our second child, Eryka, was born, and Bobbie made the decision to step away from her outside career and focus on raising our daughters. Her decision to stay home was difficult because she was educated, independent, and wanted her own career. She struggled with it to the point where it almost ended our relationship. She even harbored some resentment for a while. Eventually, it became a role she embraced wholeheartedly.

After a few years in South Carolina, I was tapped on the shoulder again, this time to move to California for promotion to Human Resources Manager. Fortunately, I learned my lesson the first time, so I knew to communicate about the opportunity with Bobbie on the front end before making any commitments.

I promised her there would be more opportunities for the kids and a lovely house with a swimming pool. So off to California we went.

As we moved from place to place, moving upward and laterally within the company, we were able to put our girls in the best schools and social environments to be successful, which was such a blessing. And as we relocated, we enjoyed traveling, exploring, and adventuring out to new places as a family—we had a lot of fun!

During my time in California, I had to start traveling a lot for work because I was in charge of six different manufacturing facilities and three distribution centers. One tough pill to swallow was the realization that when I was out of town, I missed a lot of school and extracurricular activities, and all those little day-to-day encounters of family life. Life doesn't wait, and sometimes it was hard on the family that Dad was gone so much.

Sacrifices for Family

Overall, our family did love living in sunny, warm California, so when I was tapped on the shoulder yet again to return to "the frozen Tundra of Madison" (my manager's actual words), we had to have a serious family meeting. We broke out the pen and paper to list the pros and cons, the what-ifs, and everything else we could think of that would factor into the decision. Since Tiffany was 13 and Eryka was 7 at this time, we came to the decision as a family that the move was the right one to make, so I accepted. Four months later, when the school year ended, they followed me.

We re-settled into life in Madison, and two years later… you guessed it. I was tapped on the shoulder again and given the opportunity to work at our company headquarters in Illinois, bringing me as close to the top of the corporate ladder as I'd ever been. It was a lucrative position that would put me where I dreamed of being financially. But this time, since the girls were older and so much more involved in school and extracurricular activities, the cost of moving the family was even more significant than the last.

So this time, with all the pros and cons in mind, Bobbie and I decided that instead of moving the family, I would make the sacrifice and commute to Illinois on a weekly basis, leaving on Monday mornings and returning home Friday evenings.

It was a two-year sacrifice we were willing to make for the kids, but it was hard on our marriage. I felt like I was missing a lot, so there were plenty of times I second-guessed myself. Yes, financially we were in a great place, but to be honest, at times it felt like a setback for the family.

If it had not been for our very intentional efforts at effective communication and active listening, I'm not sure we would have made it. First, we focused on our communication as husband and wife, and then together as parents. We checked in daily to make sure I was involved as much as possible with parenting decisions. Then, I'd call the kids if I needed to be loving, supportive, or sometimes strict, just to make sure they were OK.

The girls were at ages where stability was critical, with Tiffany starting high school. I did not want her to miss the opportunity to develop those close, formative friendships that develop during the teenage years.

As young adults today, Tiffany and Eryka have shared that, from their perspective, moving around so much as children had its benefits, but there were also some downsides. On the positive side, it made them more adaptable, raised their emotional intelligence, and helped them understand how to read people. Tiffany said that it made her feel very flexible in most situations and taught her how to roll with the punches. She also learned how to compete with the best and the brightest, gained from lessons learned along with every new move, which helped her become better at maneuvering and adapting.

However, each time we moved, the girls had to figure out how to join new social systems, especially as teenagers. Tiffany admitted that being young and having to navigate those systems provoked feelings of anxiety that she still has to deal with on occasion even today, especially with new or unfamiliar situations.

Over the years, we realized how important it is to keep a line of communication open with the kids when they needed to talk about a particular issue or problem. Bobbie and I each had instances of being that go-to parent, depending on what was being dealt with. When you enter that season of parenting teens, be ready to be available.

Were the sacrifices we made worth it? One-hundred percent! Today Tiffany is working as a Medical Doctor at Johns Hopkins Hospital in Baltimore, MD, and Eryka is an attorney in Washington, D.C. Bobbie and I couldn't be more proud of the young women they've become. It wasn't easy, as you can tell, but yes, it was most definitely worth it.

A Little Family Advice

How would I sum up the big lessons we learned about family and career for someone early in the Career Life Cycle? To start, and you can probably guess this, we tell everyone that communication is critical, early and often. Before you get married, have a conversation about what you are dreaming of for your life and career aspirations in 2, 5, 10, or even 50 years. Make sure you're on the same page.

When you're facing a major career decision, such as an upward promotion, lateral move, change of company, or even a total change of career, prepare your partner. Don't spring it on them like I did, or say "yes" without discussing it. Be proactive, and start communicating as soon as you see the possible change coming to limit the element of surprise.

As you communicate, work at aligning your priorities as a couple and as a family. When you agree on what is most important, it's much easier to filter opportunities that may arise to determine if one might be a good fit for your family's values and priorities.

Speaking of priorities, you can forget about work-life balance; it's a myth. Your real effort should be to develop work-life integration, where you make your work fit into your life, instead of functioning like a 50/50 balance is even possible. It's not. You'll never successfully split your work time and family time straight down the middle. Another consideration that requires attention is working from home. More companies are requiring employees to work from home rather than the traditional office space, which can be challenging to say the least.

Finally, as you're making a decision about whether to join a particular company, no matter where you are in the Career Life Cycle, always do your research to find out how that company treats the families of its employees. It's important to know if the company supports your family's values and beliefs. Do the company's values and priorities align with yours?

And one final gut check for you: if you say family is your priority, don't compromise on that. Put the phone down. Turn the computer off. Spend time with them. The days are long, but the years are short.

The bottom line is, for most of us, family is a significant factor in our career decisions and life fulfillment, and that's how it should be. The key is to intentionally integrate the two in a way that fully supports both career and life during every stage.

The Life Fulfillment Framework: Family

STAGE 1—EXPLORATION

✓ **Tip 1:** If you're married, be intentional and discuss your family growth plans so you can know you are on the same page.

✓ **Tip 2:** Before marriage, discuss relocation. If already married, have that conversation now before you get asked to make a move.

✓ **Tip 3:** Find a family support group like daycare, church, or other social outlets.

✓ **Tip 4:** Discuss who will be the primary childcare person. Will both parents be working? In home or in an office? Is childcare help needed?

✓ **Tip 5:** Keep your family relationships front and center, even in the midst of important career challenges and demands. Remember, the company doesn't love you, but your family does.

STAGE 2—ESTABLISHMENT

✓ **Tip 1:** Support and understanding from your spouse is critical. This means clear, two-way communication about expectations. Show that you're listening to their needs, too.

✓ **Tip 2:** This can be a chaotic time. Plan for how you're going to navigate the chaos. Build a support group and some type of outlet to just be a family.

STAGE 3—ELEVATION

✓ **Tip 1:** Before committing to a relocation, sit down with your family and lay out all the pros and cons of such a move. If the cons outweigh the pros, you may need to consider other options.

✓ **Tip 2:** Calendarize your family priorities. Treat those appointments just as seriously as you do business meetings and other appointments.

STAGE 4—ENRICHMENT

✓ **Tip 1:** Make a family bucket list of things you all want to do or enjoy now that you have the means. Then choose one and put it on the calendar.

STAGE 5—EXIT

✓ **Tip 1:** Communicate with your spouse and/or family members constantly. Everyone should know the master plan. There should be no surprises at any point in this process.

CHAPTER TWO

FINANCIAL

I was a newly-hired Operations Supervisor with Oscar Mayer, fresh out of the military, when I received a call from John and Tom, two colleagues at the plant. The Plant Manager had assigned them to coach and train me. Neither had a college degree; however, both had over fifteen years of service with the company and were subject-matter experts in the meat production industry.

They asked if I was going to attend the town hall meeting later that day to learn about financial planning, personal investments, and 401k's. They also asked me what percentage of my salary I was investing in the company 401k.

I didn't know what to say, so I remained quiet. To be honest, I didn't know anything about 401k's and wasn't investing *any* money. Even though I had a savings account, I was living paycheck to paycheck and basically spending money as fast as I was making it. Apparently, and ironically, I was failing miserably at keeping up with the Joneses.

The topic of investing and saving became real to me that day. The guest speaker, a certified financial advisor, provided examples of how investing as little as 3% of my salary could lead to a huge nest egg and potential financial freedom over the course of a 20-year Career Life Cycle. As I looked around the room, it seemed as though someone flipped a light switch on in my brain. I understood the financial possibilities and became totally committed to becoming financially free.

The truth is, a large number of people today, if not most, struggle to make ends meet. In addition, statistics show a racial disparity gap exists when it comes to retirement savings. The average white family has over $130,000 in retirement savings, versus only $19,000 for black families. At that time, I was determined not to become a statistic.

Early the next day, I walked into the Human Resources Manager's office and asked to speak with the Benefits Specialist. I immediately enrolled in the company's 401k plan and started investing 3% of my salary. Eventually, 3% was increased to 30% over the course of my career. In most cases, instead of spending my annual salary increases, I simply increased the percentage of my 401k.

The commitment that I made to myself to save and invest required exceptional discipline and unprecedented professional maturity, which was mastered over time. And it paid off in a huge way when it was finally time to exit my career.

Start Small. Start Now.

When we first got married, Bobbie was working, and I was in the military. We had two separate bank accounts, and yet it seemed like the money was evaporating. What we quickly learned was that when a family has one unified account, it can be managed better. With two accounts, there are going to be some leaks. When we began to take care of our finances out of one account, we started to see a light at the end of the tunnel because we developed a sound spending structure.

I recognize that it is a trend among Millennials and younger generations to maintain separate accounts, with each partner contributing certain amounts to a family fund. While I understand the reasoning, I still would encourage a married couple to combine resources. When we did so, it forced us to be open about everything. We had to learn to trust each other and navigate the challenges of wants versus needs. It's more difficult to save and invest when the majority of a family's finances are separated.

If it's a level of autonomy in spending that you desire, consider setting up separate accounts for fun money, as opposed to primary money. Making a small deposit to each partner's account every week or two still affords the opportunity for some discretionary personal spending without compromising the family's resources.

But be careful with that discretionary spending! When I went off to war, I received hazardous duty pay. That meant I was making a lot of tax-free money. But while I was out there on the battlefield, it got real and rough. My life almost came to an end at least three times. I promised myself that if I ever placed my feet back on US soil, I would buy myself a nice car. Thank God, I made it back alive. To keep the promise I made, I went ahead and bought myself that car. To this day, I hate to say I did it, but because I made myself a promise, I felt like I owed it to myself.

While I was gone, Bobbie had saved a lot of money. She tried to talk me out of getting the car. I really put up a good argument though. Finally, with her reluctant consent, I bought a brand-new, 1990 Black Porsche 911. *What was I thinking?!*

She justified the purchase in her mind by telling herself that we were doing well at the time; we were young and could recoup the money that we had saved. I think we put $8,000 down on the car, which cost around $30,000. Back then, that was a lot of money for a car!

It didn't take long for me to realize the car was a liability that placed a financial burden on us. A Porsche is a *nice-to-have*, but not a *must-have*. But I looked at the whole thing as a learning experience. From that point on, every car we had, we kept at least 10 years.

After I left the military and was recruited to work for Oscar Mayer in Wisconsin, our lack of planning nearly put us in deep financial trouble. One of the appeals of this new job was that I would make more money—significantly more. However, we failed to take into account that we got additional money in the military for certain costs of living, like rent, groceries, etc.

We weren't factoring in any of that, so when we moved to Wisconsin and got my first paycheck, Bobbie said, "I think they underpaid you! You need to go to HR and ask where the rest of your money is."

So, I dutifully went to HR and asked, "Can you make sure my paycheck is right?" They did all the calculations, and guess what? It was right! I gave them my military pay stub and my Oscar Mayer pay stub to compare, and they told me I didn't take into consideration state taxes and the additional military stipend I received every month. Lesson learned.

We thought we were about to live the high life, but in reality, we went backward financially in the move. Because we had overestimated our finances coming in, we had issues paying the bills. Although we stumbled coming out of the gates, we learned from it. I learned to research the cost of living in the next place we moved, and for every move thereafter, which wasn't an easy task back then. Now, you can find a ton of websites featuring cost of living comparisons for everything from gas to utilities to the housing market, so you can make an informed decision.

On our next move to South Carolina, I made a different financial mistake: I failed to factor in whether my wife would be able to find employment in a new location. Bobbie was working for American Family Insurance at their headquarters office in Madison, Wisconsin, so she had to give up her job, relocate, and try to find another job that fit her career experiences and degree. I simply assumed it would all work out. When it didn't, we were once again struggling, living paycheck to paycheck.

It all came to a head one summer when we were driving from South Carolina to Mississippi, bringing our daughters to see their grandparents and extended family. While driving, the car broke down. At this point, we had three credit cards, two of which were maxed-out. There was just enough credit on the third card to get the car fixed, and we still had to stay somewhere overnight. That's when it hit us that we couldn't keep living that way. We needed some financial margin.

We dropped the kids off, drove back to South Carolina, then sat down and looked at our finances. Here we were, two finance majors who were failing miserably. We wrote down every bill that we had, every single expense. Then we wrote down the revenue coming in and realized we were falling short. We decided that if we consolidated our bills, getting a consolidation loan from USAA, we would be better positioned to pay the bills and put us back in the green on a month-to-month basis. The process forced us to sit down and analyze money coming in and money going out, and think about options in an intentional way. We both agreed that the best option was to take out that loan and pay off the bills. That structure actually helped us become debt-free over time. Every year we would decide which one or two bills we were going to pay off, typically the ones with the highest interest rates first, and then we would cut up that credit card.

We did take a small step backward when we moved from California back to Wisconsin. We wanted to buy a new home and needed $50,000 for a down payment. At that career stage, we didn't have a lot of savings, but we had a lot in my 401k. I definitely do not recommend doing that now, but we went into our 401k and took out the money to use as a downpayment on our home in Madison. We took a step back, but eventually made money on the sale of the home and paid back our 401k.

Years later, when it came time for Tiffany to go to college, we didn't have enough money saved to cover her costs. When we first had Tiffany, the friends and colleagues we met early in our marriage talked about how they set up college funds for their kids. So we set up a 529 savings account through USAA with $50 a month. We knew it wasn't enough to have a big impact, but we started small and felt good about it. Every year we put more and more into the account. And that's the key: it's important to start small rather than not to do anything. You have to start somewhere.

Luckily, Tiffany earned an academic scholarship. We were in that middle stage of our career, and just beginning to see some financial light, so we couldn't give her the same financial support we were later able to give her sister. While Eryka didn't get a scholarship to the school she chose, by that time we had saved enough money to pay for her schooling. She was able to go to school without a student loan, which we were glad about.

The lesson learned here is to start early—save and invest as aggressively as you can, so you will be fully funded when the time comes. During your journey, you will eventually understand that it's not where or how you start; what matters is where and how you finish.

Ask for Help

As I shared in the beginning of this chapter, my 401k savings efforts started at the beginning of my civilian career, when I was barely making ends meet. But I was convinced that getting started was vitally important, so I began with a small contribution of around 3%.

Five years later, when I was in California, I reviewed my 401k financial statement: *WOW! That's a lot of money!* I hadn't actually realized how quickly a 401k would grow when properly managed, even with such a small initial investment.

Bobbie and I came to realize that we could really work toward a comfortable future—and maybe even early retirement. So from then on, every time I got a promotion or a pay raise (usually 2.5 - 3%), I wouldn't spend the money. We would just add it to the 401k. By doing so, we never missed what we never had. We lived below our means but we never felt the lack. We continued saving in this way until eventually 25 - 30% of my salary was being invested by the time I retired at age 53. I am not suggesting that everyone can afford to invest 25 - 30% of their salaries into a 401k or Retirement Fund. However, I am recommending that you set a lofty goal to invest the maximum percent allowed as early as possible in your career.

I believe that financial literacy has a direct correlation with financial success, especially when it's learned and put into practice early in your career. However, financial literacy among African Americans is low, which is primarily due to significantly lower upward economic mobility. African

Americans make up 13 percent of the U.S. population and constitute a critical segment of our economy. Yet financial literacy gaps exist across this demographic regardless of gender, age, income level, or degree of education. In my conversations with those older and wiser colleagues who were further down the road than I was, I came to understand the importance of bringing in someone who is completely versed in financial literacy and options.

As a result, in 2003 Bobbie and I decided to hire a financial advisor in California before we went back to Wisconsin. By that point my salary was strong, and I was getting great bonuses and stock in the company. Because we didn't know on our own how to get the greatest return on our investments and prepare for retirement, we hired an advisor with Ameriprise Financials. Not only did we enhance our knowledge of investment and financial planning, but we also opened accounts for our daughters and educated them on the importance of financial literacy. It was the best decision we could have made.

When you're ready to do the same, probably somewhere in the Elevation stage of the Career Life Cycle, start by asking around in your network for recommendations. We were fortunate to find someone who was well-grounded, certified, and entrenched in the community, but we interviewed three possible advisors before making our decision. Make sure to choose someone you can trust who has a history of being successful and honest and who works with a reputable company.

The Life Fulfillment Framework: Financial

STAGE 1—EXPLORATION

- ✓ **Tip 1:** Develop a financial plan. Start small so you won't become overwhelmed.
- ✓ **Tip 2:** Start saving for retirement, even if it's a small amount. Get in the habit now and leverage any matching benefits your company offers.
- ✓ **Tip 3:** Learn how to budget your spending and savings. Take a course, seek a financial counselor, ask trusted family members what has worked well for them, or study for yourself how to make and keep a financial plan.

STAGE 2—ESTABLISHMENT

- ✓ **Tip 1:** Monitor spending in this stage by identifying Needs versus Wants. This is a time for short-term Wants to take a back seat to those longer-term financial goals, like homeownership. There are dozens of online apps, including bank apps, to help track this.
- ✓ **Tip 2:** Understand the company's policy around relocation and maximize it to your benefit.
- ✓ **Tip 3:** Pay attention to resale factors (location, school district, etc.) when purchasing a home if you know you likely won't be living there long-term.

STAGE 3—ELEVATION

✓ **Tip 1:** Audit your current investment in your company's retirement plan. Meet with a financial advisor to discuss how to maximize this investment.

✓ **Tip 2:** Financial splurges you make today might be better invested in your future financial freedom.

STAGE 4—ENRICHMENT

✓ **Tip 1:** Schedule some time with your spouse or significant other to discuss your thoughts and plans around the next stage of your journey. Brainstorm together all the different options you could consider, then over a period of time, reflect on what resonates best with you as your next step.

✓ **Tip 2:** As financial guru Dave Ramsey says, "Debt is dumb. Cash is king." Sure, you are earning the most you've ever earned at this point in your career, but you are that much closer to the day when you'll need it for retirement. Be smart, and only spend discretionary funds that are available after all your savings are fully funded.

STAGE 5—EXIT

✓ **Tip 1:** Know your number—the amount you need to be able to live comfortably for the rest of your life.

✓ **Tip 2:** Focus on becoming debt-free if you're not already, and don't incur additional debt through unnecessary spending, like buying a new car or other high-ticket items.

CHAPTER THREE

FEARS & CHALLENGES

E veryone experiences fears and challenges they must deal with. It's never a matter of *if* you'll have something significant to deal with or *if* things won't go as expected; it's a matter of *when*.

Sometimes these fears and challenges come from the outside world, but each of us brings our own inside baggage with us as well. These internal challenges can derail us if we aren't proactive about dealing with them. Some are physical, some emotional. Some people deal with significant family challenges that bleed into the workday; others have interpersonal issues with colleagues that make it difficult to properly perform.

These internal challenges take many forms in the Career Life Cycle and often surface in unexpected ways. For me, one of my most significant challenges crystallized when I was promoted to my first Kraft Corporate Headquarters role as Associate Director HR Global Supply Chain in March of 2006.

The new position required relocating from Madison, Wisconsin to Libertyville, Illinois. I was now responsible for strategic staffing, diversity, training, and university relations for North America, which consisted of over 29,000 employees and 60 manufacturing plants. As often happens when someone starts a new position at this level, I didn't get much help; I was simply expected to figure it out.

I had to attend a weekly, cross-functional senior leader staff meeting, which included Vice Presidents and Senior Directors. During the staff meetings, I provided updates on hiring, recruitment, and diversity in North America.

In April 2006, just a month into the new role, Mary, my new manager, asked me to provide a staffing update at the meeting and also offer a hiring forecast for the upcoming quarter. My stress and anxiety levels were rising rapidly and spinning out of control. I had been hired for the position over the objections of an individual who wanted someone else to have the job. I didn't fully realize it at the time, but that person was working against me as I got started, often undermining my efforts by withholding information or help.

So as I entered that meeting, I knew I had a lot to prove in the new role. Even though I was top talent, a high-potential and high-performing leader, I feared being embarrassed or having an anxiety attack triggered by feeling irritated, upset, and constantly on guard. Most importantly, I feared losing the job I needed to take care of my family.

In that April meeting, I was the second or third presenter. All the North America Global Supply Chain Leaders sat in the conference room around a table looking at me, the new guy. I knew some of them didn't want me to have this particular role. However, while presenting, I was confident as the subject-matter expert, comfortable, thoroughly prepared, and anticipating some difficult questions. I felt really good about my delivery and the meeting outcome. My presentation went well; however, during the Q & A session, the unthinkable happened.

Some of the questions they asked began to trigger stress and increase my anxiety levels. I felt I had been set up to fail. I could sense I was getting angry. For some reason, I felt they were targeting me and singling me out. Due to the tension with the other person who wanted the role, I already struggled to trust anyone because I didn't know who wanted me there and who didn't. My emotions began taking over. I could feel myself starting to lose control. I struggled to concentrate. My heart began beating faster and faster. My hands began to shake. Sweat began to drip from my brow. I felt lightheaded, like I was going to pass out. Luckily, I was able to excuse myself and get to a restroom, where I splashed cold water on my face and pulled it together. But I knew something was not right, and I couldn't control it.

I was confused by the whole experience, and lived in fear of it happening again—which it did, a few times. Years later, in December 2013, I received a diagnosis of Post-Traumatic Stress Disorder (PTSD).

What I discovered was that my personal challenge stemmed from my time in the Army during the Gulf War.

For years, I had dealt with PTSD but never knew it. I did know I could be triggered into angry outbursts for the smallest reasons, and I spent a significant amount of time and effort controlling my emotions and behavior. As a result, I often noticed I was overly nice or worked hard to stay in a pleasant or good mood because I didn't want to be triggered.

Your challenge probably looks different, but some of the key lessons and takeaways I learned from dealing with my challenge may be helpful to you as you progress through the Career Life Cycle. In sharing my PTSD story, I hope to help you to draw parallels to your own unique situations and consider ways you might best navigate them.

In general terms, mental health can significantly impact a person's career. It shapes how co-workers and senior leaders perceive you, especially those who decide the trajectory of your career and promotional opportunities. If you struggle with anything related to mental health, whether that is PTSD, anxiety, bipolar disorder, depression, OCD, ADHD, or anything else, I recommend first seeking medical help and then speaking with a trusted mentor or colleague at work *if* it would be helpful for someone there to know your situation. It isn't necessary for you to broadcast your problems widely, and in fact, in my experience, that can have negative consequences. But don't be afraid to share your challenges or ask for help from the core people you trust.

Mental health is not the only personal challenge you may have to deal with over the course of your career. It certainly isn't the only one I faced! Lack of conscience, fears, anxiety, pressures at home, physical ailments—the list is nearly endless. The bottom line is, you need to expect to encounter struggles and be prepared to acknowledge and address them. Don't bury your problems and just hope they'll get better. If left unaddressed, they will eventually undermine your Career Life Cycle and leave you feeling unfulfilled, no matter what title is on your office door.

The Life Fulfillment Framework: Fears & Challenges

STAGE 1—EXPLORATION

✓ **Tip 1:** Know that it is normal to have fears, so don't suppress or ignore them. Face them and discuss them with your spouse, trusted advisors, and mentors.

✓ **Tip 2:** Seek the help of a trained professional if you see signs of deeper emotional, relational, or mental issues. They will only increase if left unaddressed, causing more harm down the road for you and those you love.

✓ **Tip 3:** When you're embarking on any new career direction, expect to encounter a learning curve. That is normal. But if you don't expect it, the resistance you encounter may surprise and discourage you.

STAGE 2—ESTABLISHMENT

✓ **Tip 1:** Don't ignore your fears or challenges; confront them. See a therapist, doctor, or another expert who can help guide you through.

✓ **Tip 2:** Share your thoughts and feelings with your spouse or family support system so they are aware of your situation and can walk through it with you.

STAGE 3—ELEVATION

✓ **Tip 1:** No matter where you are in the Career Life Cycle, when you recognize you are struggling with a particular issue, seek help. There is absolutely no shame in speaking to a counselor, doctor, friend, or mentor.

STAGE 4—ENRICHMENT

✓ **Tip 1:** Face your fears head-on, as opposed to ignoring them or pushing them to the back of your mind. Then, take whatever steps are necessary to fully address and manage your fears.

STAGE 5—EXIT

✓ **Tip 1:** Embrace the fear or anxiety as normal. Everyone experiences it.

✓ **Tip 2:** Lean in to friends or family members who've already walked this walk, and share your feelings and concerns with them. They may be able to offer their personal perspective on how they navigated this change of life.

✓ **Tip 3:** Instead of viewing the Exit Stage as an end, view it as a new beginning, a chance for you to start all over with another version of the Career Life Cycle as you begin your next endeavor, whatever that may be.

CHAPTER FOUR

———

FAITH

In this brief section, I'll be sharing a little about my faith and how it shaped my entire career experience. My faith played an integral part in the experience, but if you would rather not hear about it, you can move to the next chapter. I'm not trying to push my own faith on you, but I would be negligent if I failed to talk about it, because I believe there will come times in everyone's career and life when only faith will see you through.

A Life-Changing Moment

December 21, 2014, was a typical Saturday morning in Libertyville, Illinois. After enjoying a cup of coffee, working out, and walking the dog, I headed out the door for my weekly visit to my local barber—and everything typical came to a screeching halt.

As I jumped into my Infiniti QX4 SUV, I reflexively grabbed my seatbelt, just like I do every other day without thinking about it. On this day, however, I heard a soft voice in my head: *Don't buckle your seatbelt.* Even now, all these years later, I still can't believe I simply dropped the seatbelt and started the car, since that is something I would never ordinarily do. But at the time, I didn't question it and just backed out of the driveway, heading down MLK Drive toward the barbershop in North Chicago.

About two-and-a-half miles from home on a four-lane boulevard, as I was crossing through a green light at an intersection, a semi-truck pulling a trailer ran the red light heading straight at my side. The same soft voice I had heard in my driveway said, *Lay down across the passenger seat. You're going to be OK. Lay down.* So I immediately threw myself all the way down and blacked out.

When I came to, I was pinned down in my sideways position in the wreckage, my SUV sandwiched beneath the trailer part of the 18-wheeler. The roof of my car was crushed and nearly completely torn off. The headrest of the driver's seat had been completely sheared off. From what seemed like far away, I could hear sirens and people saying, *I think he's dead! He's decapitated!* Miraculously, I was in fact alive, and I was rescued from my vehicle.

Because of the severity of the crash, I was rushed into an ambulance and immediately transported to the nearest hospital, where they put me through numerous x-rays and CT scans. Incredibly, I had nothing broken, no cuts—not even a scratch!

A police officer who came to the hospital to discuss the crash told me, "An angel was with you today." She explained that if I had been buckled—like I am literally every time I get into my car—I would have died. The seatbelt would not have allowed for me to lay down across the passenger seat.

I believe it was divine intervention that preserved me that day. I believe it was my faith and relationship with God that saved my life. On that particular day, it wasn't my time. There was more for me to do.

Only Faith

Going back as far as I can remember, faith and church were important to my family. My grandparents were devout Christians. My dad even became a pastor. For us, church was not just on Sunday; it was several times during the week. We prayed at home often as a family. I went to Bible study, choir rehearsal, worship services—church life was just part of our daily life.

I gave my life to God at a very early age, so by the time I left home for college, and then later in the military, I was pretty well-rooted in my faith foundation. There were times in the Army when I started to feel challenged by some of the hardships and the obstacles I was encountering, to the point that I felt like I needed some help.

When I'd call home to my mom and dad to express my frustrations, they'd ask, "Where's your faith? Have you been to church?" I'll admit that when the going got tough, I had strayed away, but their nudging got me back on track. I started going to church again consistently. My faith really guided my walk of life. The challenges and obstacles became easier because I knew someone was with me; God was watching over me. I knew I was going to be safe and felt like my life was being used for a purpose.

Leaning into Faith

I believe God guided my corporate career path, too. By 1994, after leaving the Army and beginning employment with Kraft in Madison, Wisconsin, Bobbie and I were struggling to make ends meet. We were living paycheck to paycheck, primarily due to my poor career and job-change planning. As a result, my marriage was shaky. Frankly, it seemed the end of our marriage was near.

Finally, one day I got to the breaking point. I made up my mind to give things another few days, and then I would just have to quit my job and start a new career. Later that night, I prayed and asked God to give me the strength to endure my challenges and give me the wisdom to make the right decision for my family. A week later, I was promoted from Operations Supervisor to Financial Analyst. I gave God all the glory and thanks.

In 1997, I was working in a Senior Financial Analyst position in South Carolina. My performance was outstanding, and I was considered to be a top talent in the company. However, because I wanted to inspire others and assist them in their professional development and career aspirations, Human Resources was the field that I really needed to be in.

I knew I couldn't reach my greatest potential and live my career journey to the fullest while in a Finance role. Even though I liked the prestige of being a Senior Financial Analyst, my heart and passion just weren't in that particular field. Even so, I wasn't seeking a career change. And at that time, it was unheard of to change your career path from Finance to Human Resources.

I prayed and asked God to work it out for me. Whatever direction and career He wanted me to pursue, that's what I would do. A few days later, Lyle, the Plant Manager, called me into his office, and, out of the blue, asked me to take on a special project for three months. He wanted me to lead an HR Recruiting Project focused on hiring Spanish-speaking Food Scientists and Engineers. I completed the project, and because of the great results, I was asked if I wanted to change my career from Finance to Human Resources. The rest of the story is the history of my career.

In 2012, Kraft split into two separate companies: Mondelez International and Kraft. All employees were assigned to one of the two companies. It was out of most employees' control; someone higher-up had already made the decision. However, I was one of the very few senior leaders who had the opportunity to select which company I wanted to join.

All of my long-time friends and colleagues were assigned to Kraft, which is where the old and dying products were assigned. Kraft was the only company that I had worked for, and it was all I knew. For those reasons, it was where I really wanted to go. On the other hand, Mondelez International, which was really Nabisco along with other international products, was a new company with vibrant brands.

One night, I prayed and asked God to give me the wisdom to make the right decision, "But better yet," I said, "God, let

Your will be done." A soft voice said, *It is time to move on. Let the past go and embrace the future.*

My heart was heavy, and I didn't want to let go, but I had to. A few days later, I officially joined Mondelez International and eventually retired from the company. However, Kraft was soon acquired by Heinz and experienced a massive layoff. All of my long-time friends and colleagues lost their jobs; fortunately, most of them later landed jobs with other companies across the country.

This incident required me to step out in faith in a huge way, yet it persuaded me again that I could trust God to lead me.

Don't get me wrong, the biblical adage is true: Faith without works is dead. God is first in my life, and I didn't get to the top by myself, but I busted my rear to work hard. And my faith kept me grounded. Without it, my family and I would not have recognized that we have been so richly blessed over the years in every aspect of our lives.

My faith is still a top priority. I start every day reading from scripture or a daily devotion. I pray and self-reflect often during the day. I believe having deeply-rooted faith is key to success in life. In fact, I have anchored my life's work on the lesson found in Matthew 25:23 (ESV): "His master said to him, 'Well done, good and faithful servant. You have been faithful over a little; I will set you over much. Enter into the joy of your master.'"

I pray you lean into your faith for inspiration and encouragement on your own career journey, especially for those times when the going gets tough.

The Life Fulfillment Framework: Faith

STAGE 1—EXPLORATION

✓ **Tip 1:** Connect with a community of like-minded people who share your faith. For me, that was a local church where we not only got support for our faith but also developed relationships that made us stronger.

✓ **Tip 2:** Have a daily routine designed to keep your faith focused and strong. Develop habits of prayer, meditation, or renewal that will keep you strong when the going gets tough in your career.

STAGE 2—ESTABLISHMENT

✓ **Tip 1:** You may be tempted to disengage from your faith, but if you do, it's going to expose you to more fears, lead you to fall into bad habits, get more out of tune with your family, and live in a state of overwhelm.

STAGE 3—ELEVATION

✓ **Tip 1:** Don't neglect your faith and spiritual matters during this hectic, high-pressure season. Instead, lean into it and let it grow.

STAGE 4—ENRICHMENT

✓ **Tip 1:** Make a difference in the lives of others and for the business. I can honestly say I made a difference for direct reports, the team, and the company. I nurtured, developed, mentored, and sponsored some amazing talents, five of whom are currently in Vice President roles in different companies.

STAGE 5—EXIT

✓ **Tip 1:** Trust God and His promises. Jeremiah 29:11(NIV) says: "For I know the plans I have for you," declares the LORD, "plans to prosper you and not to harm you, plans to give you hope and a future."

CHAPTER FIVE

FRICTION—DIVERSITY, EQUITY & INCLUSION

I returned to Madison, Wisconsin for the second time in July of 2003. I had been in charge for nearly a year when several positions became vacant in my department, one of which was an Associate Human Resources Manager that would report directly to me. I had an acute awareness of the lack of diversity in management positions across the company, and I recognized this was finally an opportunity to hire a person of color, but I refused to settle for anyone less than the best. One thing was non-negotiable: the candidate had to meet the job qualifications *and* be the right fit for the position.

Several internal and external candidates applied for the position. During the interview process, members of the Leadership Team called and emailed me on different occasions. They strongly recommended—and sometimes demanded— who I needed to hire for the position. Of course, the people who they recommended were their close friends. Some didn't even have college degrees.

One candidate I encountered was a black woman who had over ten years in the company and an excellent performance record. I met with her to discuss the position and to learn more about her experiences, successes, challenges, and career aspirations. It only took a few minutes for me to suspect she was the right person for the job. We then had an extensive conversation regarding expectations, leadership, agility, integrity, values, and accountability.

Before I offered her the position, she said, "Charlie, I understand that this is an important decision. I'm asking you for an opportunity to prove myself. I promise not to disappoint you, the Leadership Team, or the employees." I could sense her deepest sincerity. I clearly understood she was in the minority on two counts: black *and* a woman. Nevertheless, she was eminently qualified and needed someone to give her an opportunity and believe in her abilities.

That moment became an epiphany. I realized that at different stages in my career, someone believed in me, gave me a chance, placed a bet, and invested in my career. The time had come to seize the moment and pay it forward, level the playing field, and leave a legacy, not just for this person but for other people of color who would come after me. My decision made the company a better place.

I have friends from all races and orientations, so it's important for me to address diversity, inclusion, unconscious biases, micro-inequities, and microaggressions in today's workplace, not only through my personal lens as an African American man, but also through the lenses of others.

Overcoming Biases

While working in Corporate America, I learned that working hard didn't teach me how to advocate for myself nor promote my accomplishments. I learned early in my career not to take a passive approach. At times, I had to be my own advocate. Yet the indisputable reality is that you can work hard and advocate for yourself all day long, but if you are a minority, you're often going to face additional barriers. Today's Diversity and Inclusion programs are working hard to eliminate those barriers, but there's still a long way to go.

I think race was a factor in my career when I started in 1993 with Kraft. However, I made up my mind not to let my ethnicity, color, or the company define me. I made it my mission to outwork and outshine everyone. In most cases, I was the first one in the office and the last one to leave.

For the most part, people in my circle embraced diversity; we were raised in diverse communities and had a progressive mindset. For example, one of my close white male friends was the Plant Manager in California. We discovered we both came from humble beginnings: him from the projects in Brooklyn, New York, and me from rural Mississippi. We both worked hard to get our positions.

While he acknowledged that, as a white male, he likely had fewer obstacles to deal with, he did find himself feeling frustrated and overlooked when the company began to embrace diversity hiring as a top priority. However, he shared with me that he learned to focus on what he could control and to give up worrying about things beyond his control. That was wisdom I took to heart and returned to again and again.

Even to this day, it's some of the best wisdom I can give people who think the deck is stacked against them—focus on what you can control, like the people you choose to surround yourself with and interact with, the effort you put into your performance, and so on.

Legal Action

Obviously, discrimination in the workplace for any of the above reasons is not legal. However, that doesn't mean it doesn't happen. If you feel discriminated against, how can you actually be proactive when you're feeling like it could be a potential issue?

First, speak with your manager *if* that manager was not the offender, accuser, or enabler. If you don't see positive results, speak with a member of Human Resources or the Ombudsman whom you trust. I emphasize the trust part because, the reality is, they are people, too, with their own biases and existing relationships in the company. If that doesn't resolve the problem, you could always take your issue up with the EEOC (Equal Employment Opportunity Commission) or the Department of Human Rights in your state.

I would also advise doing what a colleague from many years ago taught me: if you seek promotional opportunities, spend your time and energy focusing on what you can control. There is discrimination in the workplace, some intentional and some not. Almost everyone has to deal with it to some extent.

You can choose to expend all your energy fighting the battle but losing the war, and sometimes it *is* the battle to fight, but other times, it may be best to change companies or careers and find an organization that will value what you bring to the table. You should research and understand your current or potential employer's Diversity and Inclusion goals, as well as how senior leaders are held accountable if the goals are not achieved.

If you choose to fight the discrimination battle, be prepared with facts and data. You will get nowhere with phrases like, "They basically said..." or "I've been there longer." Discrimination is fought with facts and details, not emotion. Take good notes about your daily interactions to have a written record to rely on.

Understand that most career moves or promotions are not based on race/gender/age/sexuality, etc. Usually, it's because of who you know, the relationships you have, or the network you've developed. So, get to know some people who can help you get to where you want to go.

You cannot change or control what others do. You cannot change or control what others say. You cannot change or control how others treat you. However, you have complete control over how prepared you are for your work, how well you do your work, and for whom you work. If you are not appreciated for who you are where you work, take your talents elsewhere. Remember *you* are the CEO of *your* career.

The Life Fulfillment Framework: Friction

STAGE 1—EXPLORATION

- ✓ **Tip 1:** Accept the fact that you can't control everything.
- ✓ **Tip 2:** Don't be quick to assume you didn't get promoted because of a diversity issue. After decades in the corporate world, I know most people don't think that way. Do a thorough self-assessment first to see what areas you have to learn and grow before assuming the worst of others.
- ✓ **Tip 3:** If you do conclude you are facing real diversity issues from others, find a mentor to talk to about your concerns, preferably someone outside of the workplace.
- ✓ **Tip 4:** The people in your own peer group may not be the best people to talk to about this because they can simply become an echo chamber.

STAGE 2—ESTABLISHMENT

- ✓ **Tip 1:** Seek experiences that require you to step outside of your comfort zone, including relocating to a different city/state or seeking an assignment that requires you to work with different ethnic/multi-cultural groups.

✓ **Tip 2:** Cultivate friendships and relationships—in and out of work—to include people who don't look like you, think like you, speak like you, vote like you, etc. Keep an open mind.

STAGE 3—ELEVATION

✓ **Tip 1:** Look to HR to make sure you have a diverse group of candidates to select from when you're making hiring decisions.

✓ **Tip 2:** Inclusion doesn't have a color or gender; it's all about including everyone, bringing everyone along, which is equally as important as diversity. Look for opportunities to help each and every member of your team reach their full potential.

STAGE 4—ENRICHMENT

✓ **Tip 1:** There is no age limit on learning, so continue to learn and stay on top of the trends in your industry.

✓ **Tip 2:** If you believe your expertise would serve a niche in another company, don't be afraid to explore that option!

✓ **Tip 3:** Become a subject-matter expert.

STEP 5—EXIT

✓ **Tip 1:** Look into activities geared towards retirees in your area. You'll be amazed at what goes on during the week that you never knew about when you were busy in the corporate world.

✓ **Tip 2:** Commit to a volunteer engagement that requires you to be in a certain place at a certain time each week. This will give similar predictability to your schedule as you are accustomed to from your 9 - 5 workdays.

CHAPTER SIX

A FINAL THOUGHT

Life is a journey, not a destination. This journey requires you to pursue self-fulfillment and make decisions at critical junctures based on the situation, your priorities, and your values. Over the years, I have learned that having a successful career is meaningless if it means giving up on having a healthy balance in other areas of life.

Following the principles I've laid out in this Life Fulfillment Framework has brought me a happy and long-lasting marital relationship, meaningful relationships with my daughters, special friendships, financial security, a profoundly deep faith, and yes, a rewarding career.

I sincerely desire that you would find your version of this work-life integration, too.

ABOUT THE AUTHOR

Charles L. Jones (US Army Captain, Veteran) is principal of C&B HR Consulting and a seasoned Human Resource Executive with over 25 years of experience in Human Resources and Manufacturing Operations in Fortune 500 companies like Kraft and Mondelez International. He and his team provide human resources strategies and solutions to a wide range of businesses and nonprofits, including Intel, YWCA, and Millennium Corporation.

Learn more at cbhrconsulting.com.

This work reflects the author's present recollections of his experiences over time. Occasionally, dialogue consistent with the character or nature of the person speaking has been supplemented. Some names and characteristics have been changed out of a respect for privacy, and some events have been abridged. Names, characters, places, and incidents are based on the author's memories, where others may have conflicting memories. The intent of this work is to encourage the reader to move forward in their career and life, no matter the adversity or obstacles that come their way.